How to Stop being Bullied -

A Kids' Guide

First published in 2013 by CreateBooks New Zealand

Text © Ann Neville, 2013

Illustrations © Ann Neville, 2013

National Library of New Zealand Cataloguing-in-Publication Data

---

Title:	Batjack
Author:	Ann Neville
Publisher:	CreateBooks
Address:	www.createbooks.co.nz
	info@createbooks.co.nz
Format:	Paperback
Publication Date:	2013
ISBN:	9781492108788

Cover and inside illustrations by Scott Pearson
Visual Evolution: www.visualevolution.co.nz

How to Stop being Bullied -
A Kids' Guide

by Ann Neville

How to Stop being Bullied –
A Kids' Guide

This book addresses the following questions:

1. What is bullying?

2. Who gets targeted and why?

3. What does it feel like to be bullied?

4. Who can help?

5. How can kids bully-proof themselves?

6. What do other kids suggest?

7. What can be done about cyber bullying?

8. What if it's an adult who's doing the hurting?

9. What can witnesses do?

10. What do kids need to know about bullies?

11. Do the bullies themselves need help?

12. What is the key ingredient of a safe world?

What is bullying?

Bullying is *repeated* acts of hurting someone either physically or mentally or emotionally.

What do bullies do best?

hit   punch   kick   tease   push   pull   pester   brag

taunt   harass   play mind games   frighten   heckle

insult   annoy   gossip   bother   hurt   threaten   torment

ridicule   trip   pinch   act violent   intimidate

Sound familiar? They all have something in common – they are hurting you by trying to make themselves more powerful than you.

And it's not just kids that get bullied either.

It can be: kid to kid

parent to kid

kid to parent

adult to adult

adult to kid

boss to employee

Who gets targeted and why?

- Anyone who's different – whether it's their looks, weight, accent, clothing or interests. Disabilities make some kids an easy target
- Kids who are small or young – and not so able to defend themselves
- Kids who react quickly – bullies love kids who get upset or cry easily
- Kids who *aren't* sporty or kids who *are* sporty
- Kids who *aren't* brainy or kids who *are* brainy
- Anyone who is nervous or really shy

You can't win really!!!

Anyone can be bullied just by being in the wrong place at the wrong time. Sometimes the exact things that make a kid part of one group can make him a target of bullying in another. Work that one out!

So kids who are popular, smart or attractive can be victims of bullying as well.

What does it feel like to be bullied?

Bullied kids feel:

- Scared, lonely, helpless and hopeless
- Ashamed so they can't tell anyone
- Threatened with worse treatment if they tell anyone
- Excluded from those around them
- So scared they try to avoid school by faking illness, or running away from school
- Angry when anyone talks to them about what's going on in their life
- Too anxious to eat, or eat way too much
- Tearful at the thought of going to school
- So stressed that their school work suffers

Bullied kids often:

- Change their route to school, or ask their family to take them to school
- Have nightmares
- Begin wetting the bed

I bet you've got other thoughts and feelings on your list too.

Write your feelings down - but leave a space next to each feeling so you can write down how you are going to react next time someone

Who can help you?

Of course teachers and family can help. All schools should have anti-bullying policies and you should go to these people if you need to

BUT...

There are things

YOU YOURSELF

can do to stop being bullied!

Yes - YOU

Reason 1: Think about it... The bully waits behind the hedge for you. He leaps out and starts yelling at you and threatens to punch your head in. You look around and there's no-one around to help you.

Better to have some strategies up your own sleeve instead of having to rely on someone else.

Reason 2: If it's not just kids that get bullied but adults too, isn't it best to learn how **YOU** can keep yourself safe? Yeah, you don't want to be bullied for the rest of your life.

Reason 3: There are, unfortunately, lots of bullies in the world. Parents and teachers might help you with one or two. But what about the rest?

Better to learn now how to deal with them yourself... or better still, how to act so they don't target you in the first place!

Make a pact with yourself
I WILL NEVER ALLOW MYSELF TO BE A VICTIM AGAIN!

How to bully-proof yourself

You have the **right** not to be bullied,

harassed, assaulted or abused.

Remember the pact:

I WILL NEVER ALLOW MYSELF

TO BE A VICTIM AGAIN!

This is where **YOU** take control.

Will it be easy? No

Will it take some practise? Yes

Can someone do it for you? No, but they can help

Is it really possible for you to do this? **YES**

You have the choice
either

Continue to act as you have in the

past and continue to be bullied

or

Change how you react and stop being a victim.

It's important to realise that **YOU** can't change the bully (only he/she can do that) but you can change what **YOU** do. And this booklet is for you.

So what can YOU do?

Understand that the mean things that the bullies say are false. They may contain a grain of truth (after all, nobody is perfect). That grain is there to fool you into thinking the whole accusation is true, which it is not. It is important to understand this.

Think of bullying as a game, a nasty game, but never-the-less a game. And there are two people playing – the bully and you.

Stop playing this game

Here's how.

1. Get in front of a mirror when no-one else can see you and take a good hard look at yourself. Who are you? What do you really look like?

I'm not talking about things you can't change - like spots, or no muscles, or no boobs... If there are things looking back from the mirror that you don't like and can't change – get over it!!! Everyone has things about themselves they don't like.

On the other hand, if there are things you don't like and can change, get going and do it!

Work on the things you can change

e.g. Posture

Stand up straight and walk confidently

Look people in the eye

Hold your head high

Work on appearing more sure of yourself.

Practise, practise, practise in front of the mirror till it feels more natural.

**If you ACT more confident,
you'll soon FEEL more confident.**

Which of these kids is more likely to be bullied?

2. You need to practise what you'll say and how you'll say it to the bully. Stand in front of a mirror and pretend you're talking to the bully. Speak clearly and firmly. And show confidence. Practice saying the words until you feel sure of yourself.

Come up with some things to say in different situations so you're not stuck for words e.g.

- I'd like to agree with you, but then we'd both be wrong.
- No, (bully's name), don't sit down, you'll crush your brains.
- Stop, don't move. I want to forget you exactly as you are.
- May my friend's pitbull clamp his teeth on your what's-it and never let go.
- I never forget a face, but in your case I'll make an exception.
- Do you still love nature, despite what it did to you?

Well, maybe not these because then you're being as nasty as the bully!

However, using humour is a great way to diffuse a situation.
Try saying something unexpected like this instead:

Scene: The Bully says something rude about you.
You reply:
'Gee, thanks for the compliment. You've made my day,' and walk off as if it really has made you happy.

or

'You can think what you want but I am happy with the way I am.'

or

'You have your opinion and I have mine.'

or

'Hmmm... thanks for the advice. I'll consider it.'

or

...come up with a few ideas yourself.

How good are you at acting?

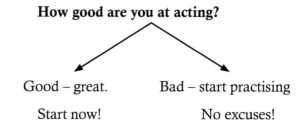

Good – great.   Bad – start practising
Start now!   No excuses!

If you ACT more confident,
You will soon FEEL more confident.

3. What do you do if the bully keeps threatening to mash you into the dirt?

When in doubt SHOUT and RUN

Shouting will take the bully by surprise and you may have a chance to get away. If there are other people there the bully will feel uncomfortable and may just scoot away.

So if someone still threatens to punch your lights out what do you do?

Best self defence? Don't be there in the first place.

Second-best self defence? Run like hell. But if you think your attacker is going to catch you, here's a couple of tips:

At the very last minute crouch down in a ball so they trip over you,

or drop some fake money...

Bullies are the greedy sort!

Third-best self defence? Pray and hope your parents

have medical insurance. Just joking!

The proper third defence is self-defence!

Learn self defence

Why? Because it instils positive discipline,

Builds character,

Improves concentration skills,

Develops fitness,

And you learn release skills that are effective if someone grabs you.

Your instructor will teach you some techniques to use **BUT ONLY IN SELF DEFENCE**, like

- Kick where it will hurt most! You know where! And the same place if your attacker is a girl. Hurts girls when you kick there too.
- If he's holding you from behind, stomp hard on his foot then swing round and elbow him under the chin.

•

- If someone grabs you from behind tying up your arms, use the edge of your foot and scrape as hard as you can down his shin.
- Lock your arm straight and push his chin up and back with your hand. With your arm locked tight you have much more leverage.

- Push your fingers or thumb into that little hollow at the base of your attacker's neck.

- Slap your hands hard over their ears. At the very least it will disorientate your attacker, at worst you'll rupture their ear drum... and that is painful!
- If all else fails, push your thumbs into your attacker's eyeballs.

Do it - Go to Self Defence Classes!

4. The last thing you need to do is this and it's

VERY IMPORTANT!

Get another piece of paper and write down all the things you are better at than the bully.

Surprised? Keep reminding yourself of all the things you know that the bully doesn't and all the things you can do better.

Bullies think they've hit the jackpot when they make you cry. Don't reward them with tears. Stay as calm as you can.

Also think of the ways you act towards other people and give yourself a pat on the back for always treating others with respect.

What do other kids suggest?

Ellie (11): Stand tall and be brave. When you're scared of another person, you're probably not feeling your bravest. But sometimes just acting brave is enough to stop a bully. How does a brave person look and act? Stand tall and you'll send the message: 'Don't mess with me.' It's easier to feel brave when you feel good about yourself!

Jamie (10): Feel good about you. Nobody's perfect, but what can you do to look and feel your best? Maybe you'd like to be more fit. If so, maybe you'll decide to get more exercise, watch less TV, and eat healthier snacks. Or maybe you feel you look best when you shower in the morning before school. If so, you could decide to get up a little earlier so you can be clean and refreshed for the school day.

Todd (12): Get a buddy (and be a buddy).
Two is better than one if you're trying to avoid being bullied. Make a plan to walk with a friend or two on the way to school or during breaks or wherever you think you might meet the bully. Offer to do the same if a friend is having bully trouble. Get involved if you see bullying going on in your school — tell an adult, stick up for the kid being bullied, and tell the bully to stop.

Sarah (9): Ignore the bully. Try your best to ignore the bully's threats. Pretend you don't hear them and walk away quickly to a safeplace. Bullies want a big reaction to their teasing and meanness. Acting as if you don't notice and don't care is like giving no reaction at all, and this just might stop a bully's behavior.

Tane (12): Stand up for yourself. Pretend to feel really brave and confident. Tell the bully "No! Stop it!" in a loud voice. Then walk away, or run if you have to. Kids also can stand up for each other by telling a bully to stop teasing or scaring someone else, and then walk away together. If a bully wants you to do something that you don't want to do — say "no!" and walk away. Bullies tend to bully kids who don't stick up for themselves. Or just start laughing – bullies *hate* that!

Justin (13): Don't bully back. Don't hit, kick or push back to deal with someone bullying you or your friends. Fighting back just satisfies a bully and it's dangerous, too, because someone could get hurt (probably you). You're also likely to get in trouble.

Alicia (8): Don't show your feelings. Plan ahead. How can you stop yourself from getting angry or showing you're upset? Try distracting yourself (counting backwards from 100, spelling the word 'turtle' backwards, etc.) to keep your mind occupied until you are out of the situation and somewhere safe where you can show your feelings.

Fleur (11): Tell an adult. If you are being bullied, it's very important to tell an adult. Find someone you trust and tell them what is happening to you. Teachers, principals and parents at school can all help to stop bullying. Sometimes bullies stop as soon as a teacher finds out because they're afraid that they will be punished. Bullying is wrong and it helps if everyone who gets bullied or sees someone being bullied speaks up.

How do you deal with cyber bullying?

Cyber bullying happens through things like Facebook, YouTube or MySpace, in chat rooms, via email and on SMS or mobile phones.

This cyber aspect is usually part of an overall bullying campaign which includes face-to-face bullying.

It is just as bad as face-to-face bullying.

Be cyber savvy

- Think about the places and sites on-line you go and the activities you're involved in. Are they safe? Are they necessary – do you really have to use them? If not, don't go there!

- Are you being responsible when using your computer and mobile phone? Make sure you **never** post or say anything that you wouldn't want the whole world (or your parents!) to see or read.

- **Don't** retaliate. **Do** keep a record of all instances of cyber bullying and **tell an adult** (and if that adult does nothing, tell another one and another one until someone does do something). Who could you tell? Your parent, teacher, guidance counsellor, police...

What if it's an adult who is hurting you or making you do things you don't want to?

Forget about dealing with it yourself. The most important thing is to tell someone. Kids should let adults know that someone is hurting them, even if it's someone really close to them that they love.

Choose someone you can trust. Tell them you need to talk about something in private. If you're not sure if it's abuse or not, you can tell the person that something happened and that you want to check to see if it is be abuse/bullying.

It takes a lot of courage to talk about this kind of thing, and sometimes it takes a while to feel strong enough to talk about it. That's OK. Just know that, in the end, telling a safe person is the **bravest** thing a kid can do. It can feel really good when a kid takes steps to stay safe and happy and stop the abuse from happening.

But what if the person threatens to do something worse if you tell on them? Or the person says it's a secret between you and them and you mustn't tell anyone else? Huh - that proves they know what they are doing is wrong.

TELL SOMEONE – NOW!

What can witnesses do?

Make a safe choice. Think about the level of risk in choosing an action before intervening. For instance, you could:

- Refuse to participate
- Tell an adult
- Take an individual stand and tell the bully what he/she is doing is NOT okay

- Encourage your friends to take a stand with you
- Be friendly toward the bully (Yes, I'm serious!)
- Help someone who is being bullied by making a group or individual decision to say to the person doing the bullying that what they are doing is not okay
- Listen to the kid who is being bullied and let them talk about how it feels
- **Doing nothing tells the bully that what they are doing is okay. That makes you part of the problem, too**.

What you need to know about bullies

There are lots of different reasons people bully.
Some reasons identified by kids are:

• They might get power and strength from bullying others

• It's a way to get known at school

• Because they are scared themselves, they try to scare others to hide their feelings

• Because they are unhappy and take it out on others

• Often bullies come from homes where the parents use physical force to make their kids behave. As a result, bullies have a lot of anger inside them

• As a way to try and fit in

Children who bully also have a right to be treated with respect.

No way, you say!

Actually, underneath it all most bullies have even higher levels of anxiety and stress and feel even worse about themselves than you do about yourself. Really!

Think about it – why else would they need to be a bully? That doesn't mean what they do is acceptable – it is definitely NOT.

But who would you rather be?
The Bully?

Someone who feels so bad about
themselves they have to bully someone
else to make themselves seem better?

or

You?

Someone who knows what they're
good at and respects and
cares about other people

Of course it's YOU! Especially now you're not playing the bully's game anymore.

Do the bullies themselves need help?

Most bullies wind up in trouble. If they keep acting mean and hurtful, sooner or later they'll have only a few, if any, friends left – usually other kids who are just like them. Kids who feel good about themselves move on and leave bullies behind.

The good news is that kids who are bullies can learn to change their behaviour. Teachers, counsellors, and parents can help. Maybe you could help by being friendly to them. Hmmm – maybe not!

In the end, whether bullies decide to change their ways is up to them. Some bullies turn into great kids. Some bullies never learn.

So it's definitely worth it for their parents and/or teachers to help bullies for two reasons:

Reason 1: So the bully can lead a happy life themselves

Reason 2: You may stop playing the victim in their bullying game but there's always someone else they can target. Better to fix the bully!

What is the key ingredient for a safe, healthy world?

Imagine if we lived a world where everyone

Respected themselves

Respected their own and everyone else's property

Respected everyone else regardless of their race/ ethnicity, age, gender, religion, abilities

Respected the environment

Do bullies respect themselves, everyone around them, their own and other people's property? Obviously not!

How about you? Do you respect yourself, everyone around you, your own and other people's property?

Respect

Good luck on your journey as a capable,

self-confident person who is never bullied!

References and Further Reading

Romain, Trevor. (1997). Bullies are a Pain in the Brain. Free Spirit Publishing Inc, USA

Time for Tolerance. By children, for children http://library.thinkquest.org/07aug/00117/bullyingconsequences.html
http://www.cyberbullying.org.nz/
http://www.kidsline.org.nz http://www.kidspot.co.nz/
http://kidshealth.org/
http://www.kiwifamilies.co.nz/articles/dealing-with-bullying/
http://www.minedu.govt.nz/
http://www.police.govt.nz/new-zealand-police-youtheducation-information
http://www.youthline.co.nz/

Telephone Help

There are telephone help lines in all countries. Check online for those relevant to you. For instance:

In Australia:
http://www.kidshelp.com.au/teens/ Call 1800551800
http://www.youthbeyondblue.com/get-help/
phone-help-lines/ Call 1300 22 4636

Telephone Help cont.

In Canada:

Kids Help Phone Call 1-800-668-6868

In New Zealand:

Kidsline Call 0800 KIDSLINE (New Zealand 0800 543 754)

What's Up Telephone counselling for 5-18 year olds.

Call (0800) 942 8787

Youthline Call (0800) 37 66 33 or email talk@youthline.co.nz

In UK

http://familylives.org.uk/ Call 08088002222

http://www.youngminds.org.uk/for_parents/ parent_helpline

Call 08088025544

In USA:

Just For Kids Hotline Call 1-888-594-KIDs

Girls and Boys Town National Hotline Call

800-448-3000 or TDD: 800-448-1833

Also by Ann Neville
Fiction

BATJACK

Thirteen year old Tom wants to audition for the school musical BATJACK, but he has a problem - A BIG ONE - Dylan, a bully and Tom's arch enemy.

"You'll pay for this," swears Dylan when Tom is cast as Batjack and Dylan as his understudy. The battle begins – fights, verbal abuse, vandalism, theft... You name it – it happens.

And so from auditions to opening night Tom and his friends, Sonny whose shoulders are spindly as a wire coat hanger and Alice with more piercings than a sieve, come up with quirky and funny ways to deal with Dylan and his mates.

But why does Dylan bully? What is his secret and can Tom and Dylan reach a compromise and manage to co-habit the same planet?

Available from:

www.createbooks.co.nz

Non-fiction

How to Bully-Proof Your Child - A Parents' Guide

What can you as a parent do to

bully-proof your child?

Are there strategies kids themselves

can use to stop being bullied?

YES!

This guide answers questions such as:

What is bullying?

Who gets targeted and why?

What are the signs your child is a victim?

What can your child do about it?

How can you help?

What can be done about cyber bullying?

What can witnesses/bystanders do?

Do the bullies themselves need help?

What is the key to providing a

safe world for your child?

Available from:

www.createbooks.co.nz

info@createbooks.co.nz

R.I.P. Cyberbullying

Cyberbullying is one of the major issues facing children, parents and educators today. However, there are many children who are NOT bullied, by cyber means or otherwise, despite appearing to be exactly the same type of child as those who are.

What makes the difference?

This is where parents/caregivers can play a significant role.

This guide addresses the following questions:

What is cyberbullying?

Types of cyberbullying

Why do some people cyberbully?

How does cyberbullying affect children?

What can parents do to PREVENT cyberbullying?

What can parents do if the child is already being cyberbullied?

What if it's your child who is the cyberbully?

What role do bystanders/witnesses play?

When should education about cyberbullying begin?

Available from:

www.createbooks.co.nz
info@createbooks.co.nz

Made in United States
North Haven, CT
20 February 2023

32889652R00022